# MIAMI

## *city of dreams*

## ALAN S. MALTZ

Text by Les Standiford

Light
Flight
Publications

Key West, Florida

The Magic City

*"Yesterday is but today's memory...*

*and tomorrow is today's dream."*

Kahlil Gibran

Orange Bowl Pageantry

# City of Dreams

Gateway to the Caribbean. Capital of South America.

The "New" New York. Magic City. City of the Future. City of Dreams.

These names and scores more, all of them coined for a city clinging to a strip of ancient coral sea-bottom hooved up eons ago between the Gulf Stream and The Everglades, known on the map and in the news as Miami. Originally an Indian settlement, an agricultural community purveying some odd root called "coon-tie", a backwater, a port for pirates and ship-scuttlers; later a 20's boom town just as quickly erased by a scourge called hurricane; after which came a period of sleepy tourism, those "Moon Over Miami" days, which, by the 1950's, gave rise to an East Coast version of Las Vegas.

Reaching Out / Reflecting Pool  *Holocaust Museum*

A little over a hundred years of boom and bust, crime and punishment, high times for tourism and low, Miami has endured it all, cycles that wax and wane like the tides that have lapped the shores of Biscayne Bay from the days long before time was invented.

Coral Castle *Florida City*

Which brings us to the true source of the world's endless fascination with Miami — its natural beauty, flora and fauna in exotic profusion, beaches combed by temperate breezes from an Atlantic riding high outside a sheltering reef, it is a physical paradise and a wellspring of living poetry. Palm, hibiscus, flamingo, bougainvillea. Anhinga, osprey, gull. Manatee, snapper, bonefish, grouper. Coral reef and hardwood hammock, mangrove, banyan, the fabled Dade County pine, so dense, the story goes, it takes two men to carry those two-by-fours. Mango, guava, lichee nut, grapefruit. Alligator, orange, lemon, lime.

All this and the many human cultures too, clustering so precariously about a ridge of "high" ground that never climbs to the height of a Greyhound bus, a fifteen mile wide strip of sand and coral that seems Nature's afterthought in a vista that is otherwise sea and sawgrass...

...that such a place could not only come to be, but thrive, playground to the world, haven to the dispossessed, chin up against the occasional hurricane and a series of social and political transformations more numerous than most American cities have seen in the history of the republic, it is no wonder that Miami captures the heart and the soul as it does. When there's trouble here, it's even more distressing in the eyes of the world, for it is trouble taking place not just anywhere, but in paradise itself.

Art on Exhibition  *Dade County Youth Fair*

It is a pleasure dome, but it is also a working city, a place of constant beginning and renewal, a place where anything can happen and often does.  It is, as it always has been, a city of dreams.

Prince of Peace  *Liberty City*

Paradise / Museum of Contemporary Art  *North Miami*

One Man's Paradise  *The Everglades*

Field of Dreams  *Homestead*

Field of Greens  *Redlands*

Marjory Stoneman Douglas

The Florida Panther *The Everglades*

Opposites Attract  *The Everglades*

Redlands

Still Life                                        Real Life

Real Still Life  *Redlands*

Harvesting  *Homestead*

Harvester *Florida City*

Twilight in Transition

City of Splendor

Miami International Airport                                              Departure

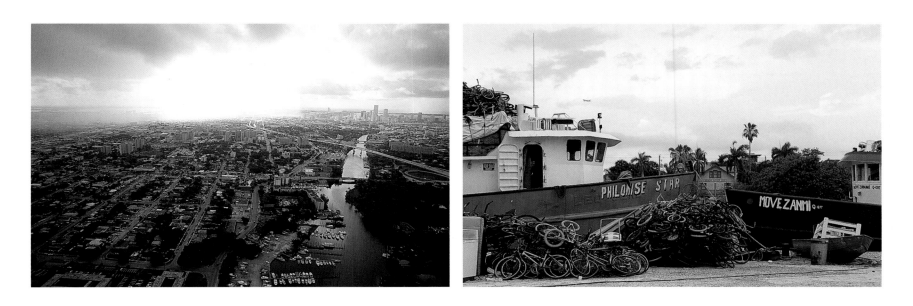

Miami River                                        Destination Haiti

Dreaming of Tomorrow *Coconut Grove*

Vernon Scott *Liberty City*

Brooms of a Different Color  *Little Havana*

Art Attack

Brickell Avenue by Night

Brickell Avenue by Night II

Brickell Avenue                                    Coral Gables

First Union Tower  *Downtown*

Quest for Clarity *Brickell Avenue*

Tropical Surroundings *Brickell Avenue*

City of the Future

City of Dreams  *Vizcaya*

Stiltsville

*"There was absolutely no escape from the sea. It was spread before you always. When you turned your back to it, you faced more of it. You woke with it, worked with it, played with it, made love with it, slept with it. Always the ocean. Always its pressure in the ears, its rippling light, its haunt."*

— from BONES OF CORAL, James W. Hall

# The Water

Aerial Perspective  *Government Cut and South Pointe*

There are other great port cities of course, and many lovely mar-
riages of city and ocean along the coastline of the United States. But perhaps in no other place does civilization mesh with sea in such  striking,
varied, and pervasive fashion as it does in Miami.  It is a fact that has not
escaped the many writers who have come to call the city home.    Contemporary novelists as diverse as

Sea Dreams  *Coconut Grove*

Hall, Carl Hiaasen,  Charles Willeford, Evelyn Mayerson, and Douglas Fairbairn have treated Miami in dis-
parate fashion, but all have written eloquently of the beauty and the influence of the water upon life in
South Florida.

North of Government Cut, the deep channel that allows ocean-going freighters and liners access
to port and maintenance facilities along the Miami River, the Atlantic has unfettered access to the broad
strand of South Beach, the famed oceanside playground with its pounding surf and palms and pristine
sands.  South of the cut, a barrier reef rises up, running all the way to Key West, and forming a protective
shield that turns the formidable breakers into wavelets more characteristic of an inland lake.  The warm,
sheltered waters of Biscayne Bay form a pleasure boater's paradise, and the mangrove-fringed shallows provide the same for fishermen.

Elements of Nature  *Card Sound Road*

The most exclusive addresses in Miami are those on man-made islands dotting the waters between the mainland and Miami Beach. Not far away, a series of uninhabited islets, created by the spoil from dredging activities earlier in the century, served in 1983 as the sites for enviro-artist Cristo to drape in miles of wavering pink, underwater cloth.

The placid bay has inspired even the wildest conceptions of developers: at one point in the 1950's, an entire community was to spring up on pilings dropped through a dozen feet of water into the silty bottom, a series of homes and weekend retreats hovering like a mirage above the shallow waters, five miles offshore and accessible only by boat. No traffic problems, no taxes, no annoying delays getting to the beach. Though federal regulations soon put an end to new construction and ensuing hurricanes were to batter the original 40 or so structures of Stiltsville mightily, several of them still remain, unlikely but obdurate, testaments to the power of this place to incite the most fanciful dreams.

*"He had been standing away from the party at the stern of the Mandalay Queen, staring eastward out to sea. The tail end of a perfect south Florida sunset, the water gone steely blue, so calm it was hard to tell where the horizon left off and the mirrored sky took over. A lone pelican up there, now, lumbering through the last of the light toward shore....Quiet Cole Porterish music, cocktail chatter like a distant rain shower for background, and a view of paradise laid out before him. This was why Florida had been invented, he was thinking...there was a blinking green buoy a half mile off to port, marking the way through the shallow waters of the bay. Beyond it, a group of strange-looking shadows shimmered, looking almost like houses floating above the water. Which is very nearly what they were.*

*"Stiltsville," he said, taking the drink. He gestured toward the horizon. "I worked out there one summer. Did you know that?" She followed his gaze. "No," she said thoughtfully, "I don't think you ever said."*

— from  DONE DEAL, Les Standiford

Wake of Light  *Biscayne Bay*

Stiltsville U.S.A.

Early Morning  *Coconut Grove*

Scenic View  *Coconut Grove*

Frog and Lizard Fountain  *Vizcaya*

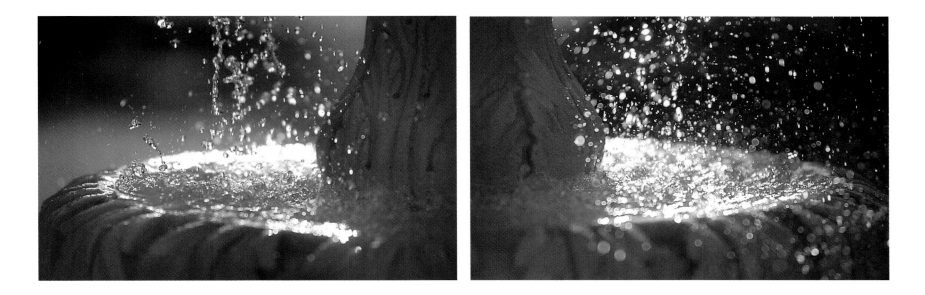

Symmetry *Coral Gables*

Serenity *South Beach*

By the Sea *South Beach*

Dinner Key

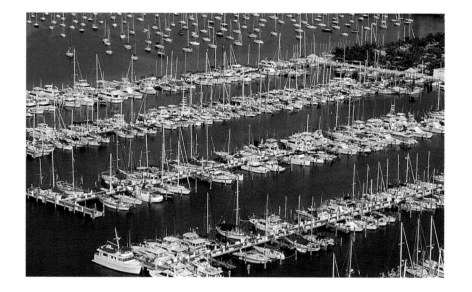

Dinner Key Marina

Port of Miami

Aerial View  *Key Biscayne*

City on the Edge

# On The Edge

The late poet Richard Hugo once told a gathering of students that he had always lived on the edge, in his profession, and life-style, even in his choice of homes on one side of the continent or the other: "it's the perfect place for the writer," he said. "Out there on the edge, looking in, where you're able to observe things more clearly."

Hugo would have loved Miami, city on the edge, on the frontier, gateway between North and South, portal to the Caribbean, entry point for seekers of the American Dream. Contemporary commentators as diverse as Joan Didion *Miami*, David Rieff *Going to Miami*, and T.D. Allman *Miami: City of the Future*, have agreed that the very future of the nation can be glimpsed from this vantage point. As New York served as bellwether for a changing America at the beginning of the century and Los Angeles did at mid-century, so Miami serves at the end of the century, as wave after wave of new, revitalizing culture sweeps ashore.

Hugo would have loved the intellectual energy of it all; but even more, he would have treasured the everyday poetry: sights, sounds, smells, tastes, and the touch of the Gulf Stream breeze, no melting pot this, but rather a rich stew, dizzying in its complexity.

Divine Interaction *Miami Beach*

There's a certain chaos to life in a city of some two million that contains a certifiable colony of most Latin American and Caribbean nations within its borders. But what a panoply of choice exists. Shops, markets, restaurants, consulates, even entire driving schools devoted not only to serving a newly arrived populace but also to offering the old-timer (someone who's lived in Miami longer than a decade) a taste of yet another culture within a twenty-minute drive.

Consider the prospect: a breakfast of *huevos rancheros* at a modest storefront restaurant that's been developed in deep South Dade by a Mexican family who came over originally to work the vast vegetable fields covering that part of the county. Take a leisurely drive through the farmlands, stop off for a fresh-picked strawberry shake and some home-baked goods at the Amish bakery that's tucked alongside a country road as remote and Rockwellian as an Iowa lane. Another half-hour and you can have lunch on bustling *Calle Ocho*, or Southwest Eighth Street, main thoroughfare of Miami's Little Havana, where veteran waitresses at any num-

ber of Cuban restaurants will guide the uninitiated through the choices toward *ropa vieja* (a shredded flank steak in a rich red sauce), or fried grouper chunks, or a chicken breast braised in lime juice, some black beans and rice and diced onion to go with that, of course, and maybe a Hautey *cerveza* or two as well, now that the once-celebrated Cuban beer is once again being produced, albeit stateside. There's time for some shopping — straw goods, native jewelry and handicrafts, even fine art — at the Caribbean-styled Bayside Market; fresh Daiquiris and u-peel-em shrimp at dockside, where you can watch the pleasure boats and the cruise liners come and go. Then, maybe a snooze in the late-afternoon sun before dinner at one of the world-class nou-velle American cuisine emporiums that dot the city and South Beach, all of it topped off by a visit to that club featuring a Rio-styled revue for a nightcap. Of course, that's just day one, and there are still another three-dozen cuisines and cultures to go.

El Rodeo *Florida City*

There can be no misunderstanding why Miami has been called America's Casablanca. In the same way that a bit of every Mediterranean culture found its way to that North African port, so has every Latin and Caribbean culture left its mark on modern-day Miami. In a similar way, Miami mixes the elegant and the raffish, the sophisticated with the casual. At one of the scores of sidewalk cafes on South Beach, a pair of leggy

News Café *South Beach*

models in bikini tops and cutoffs roller-blade up to a table, chatting in German, and plop down next to a group of suited businessmen hammering out the possibilities — in rapid-fire Spanish — of a convention hotel on that vacant property just there, at the end of Ocean Drive, where barely a decade ago, one might have snapped up a run-down pensioner's hostel for the price of an upscale automobile.

On the edge, there is always action, and there is the heat that comes with it. Where a decade ago, there was one professional sports franchise in South Florida, suddenly there have become four, and no accident that one is named for that amalgam of climatalogical factors and plain old frictional force. In a word, Miami is hot. It's a deal-maker's town, where celebrities come not only to play, but to stay, and to join the action. When Miami's venerable and striking Gusman Theater was threatened by the wrecker's ball, it was Sylvester Stallone himself who stood toe-to-toe in council chambers, pledging sufficient support to save the day. Virtually the entire professional sports community of South Florida has banded together in support of the Miami Project to Cure Paralysis, one of the leading research centers in the field.

Of course, to some, being "on the edge" leads to edginess. All those cultures colliding and sometimes sending off sparks. Nothing like a session of the county government for a lesson in pluralism, for example. But the flip side is the sense of possibility that's palpable in the Miami air. There's a freshness here, a sense that no group's firmly in charge, that your dreams are as good as anyone else's, and just as likely to come true. In Miami. On the edge.

Local Color *South Beach*

Familiar Places *Coconut Grove*

Familiar Faces  *Coconut Grove*

Wolfie's *Miami Beach*

Locals Only  *Coconut Grove*

Passing the Cup *Coconut Grove*

Morning Ritual

Heat of the Moment  *Coconut Grove*

Time Out *Coral Gables*

Cheers

Sunny Disposition *Calle Ocho*

Nature by Design

Exotic Wildlife Rescue Team  *Redlands*

Aftermath of Andrew  *Redlands*

Redlands

Solo Flight  *Hialeah Park*

Day at the Races  *Hialeah Park*

Tribute on I-95

Man of Distinction  Don Shula

Dolfans

Dan Marino

Enthusiasm *Orange Bowl '96*

In Tune *Orange Bowl '96*

End of an Era

Orange Bowl Trophy

Vizcaya

According to noted South Florida author James W. Hall, there are three major periods in Miami history: before Miami Vice; during Miami Vice; and after Miami Vice. It's a good joke of course, but like most good jokes, it contains its essential elements of truth.

While the Miami area had been settled since 1835, when a small Army outpost known as Fort Dallas was established at the mouth of the Miami River, Miami itself was not established until the end of the 19th Century. Life in those intervening years was primitive, access to the area available primarily by boat. A sizable colony of Native Americans inhabited the region, digging the native coontie and living in relative harmony with a rag-tag collection of hardy settlers.

The most affluent of those early residents included a fair number of "marine salvage experts," drawn by the frequent wrecks in the shallow waters offshore, where tropical storms and jagged reefs made for jittery summertime passage. Some of these early entrepreneurs, or land pirates, were not above finding means to augment nature's threat — a favorite tactic was to erect a phony lighthouse that would lure ships into treacherous waters. Once the ship had gone aground, the light would be doused and a rescue and salvage operation would begin, with the emphasis on the latter.

# History & Culture

Cape Florida Lighthouse *Key Biscayne*

It was not a style of life nor a sort of industry that attracted the desirable element, and a number of the local citizenry began casting about for ways to make the Fort Dallas area a more attractive place to live. As the story goes, a severe freeze dipped far south into Florida during the winter of 1895, wiping out most of the state's citrus crop. In a recurrent theme for Miami history, what was a catastrophe for many became a boon for settlers who had long campaigned that Henry Flagler extend his Florida East Coast Railroad southward from Palm Beach to their rugged outpost on Biscayne Bay. Julia Tuttle, it is said, came up with a lobbyist's stroke of genius, sending Mr. Flagler a bundle of Miami orange boughs with their blos-

soms untainted by frost. Flagler got the point. With the promise of sizable tracts of land in exchange for his trouble, he was moved not only to extend his tracks to Mrs. Tuttle's doorstep but to build a town about it as well. Miami it was named, after the tiny river that spilled into Biscayne Bay.

Over the quarter century to follow, Miami boomed as a tourist des-tination, and Flagler's success had fueled the dreams of many a fellow vision-ary. John Collins, to be immortalized by the fabled avenue that still bears his name, bought up some seven square miles of barrier island land just off-

Grapefruit *Coral Gables*

shore, and by pumping sand from the bottom of Biscayne Bay to fill out its rugged contours, transformed that nearly valueless agricultural acreage into a city that became Miami Beach, the densest collection of hotels and condominiums this side of the Cote d'Azur. George Merrick looked at Miami and Miami Beach, and seeing that they were good, determined that, city-wise, he could go them one better.

Merrick bought up vast swathes of soggy land south and west of the mainland city, planned meticu-lously (the deed and zoning restrictions are regarded to this day as among the most demanding in the coun-try), and built grandly; dredging, filling, cutting canals, quarrying rock, laying out grand plazas, huge foun-tains, and imposing public facilities, including the enormous Venetian Pool, one of the most fanciful and strik-ing examples of its kind, with its sprawling lagoons and exotic grottoes carved from the native coral rock.

Venetian Pool  *Coral Gables*

Venetian Pool *Coral Gables*

Coral Gables, Merrick was to call his city, including within its boundaries imposing boulevards lined with mansions in the Mediterranean-Revivalist style, country clubs, golf courses, sprawling parks and one of Merrick's most inspired creations, the University of Miami. The Biltmore Hotel was the architectural and social focal point of the planned community. Merrick enticed Paul Whiteman to play in its grand ballroom, Esther Williams to perform aqua ballet in its 22,000 square foot pool, and the Duke and Duchess of Windsor to sleep in its beds. Among those guests rubbing elbows with the Duke and Duchess were Judy Garland, Bing Crosby, Ginger Rogers, various Roosevelts and Vanderbilts, and even Al Capone, who was said to favor a certain suite on the thirteenth floor. Guests splashed in the largest hotel pool anywhere, played tennis and golfed on the grounds, dined extravagantly, and afterward, rode gondolas shipped from Venice up and down the canals that circled the fairways.

It was emblematic of the Jazz Age and of the heady feelings that fueled the Florida land boom, as the craze to cash in on Florida was known. The frenzy to join the party led to the investment of as much as $100,000,000 a year at the apex. But the party couldn't last forever, of course, and what the natural cycles of speculation and disappointment and the devastating hurricanes of 1926 and 1928 didn't finish (downtown

Miami was virtually destroyed), the Great Depression did. Flagler's once grand railroad was forced into receivership. George Merrick was driven into penniless retirement in a Florida Keys fishing camp. Miami became a working man's town, Miami Beach a retiree's haven, and Coral Gables a quiet, genteel suburb, the once-grand Biltmore transformed into a Veteran's Administration Hospital.

Bathed in History  *Coral Gables*

George Merrick House  *Coral Gables*

Biltmore Hotel  *Coral Gables*

Ceiling / Everglades Suite  *Biltmore Hotel*

In keeping with history however, World War II was to be a godsend for Miami, which became a major training center for U.S. servicemen. Hotels that hadn't seen guests in years were suddenly bursting at the seams with trainees. The trainees were to remember those moon-kissed sandy beaches and tropical ocean breezes, and enough of them returned after the war to revitalize the city. The 50's brought a rebirth of big-time tourism to

Plaza of Cuban Patriots *Little Havana*

Miami Beach, when its fabled Vegas-styled hotels rose up, the Fontainebleau and the Doral among them, where Gleason, Sinatra, and the Rat Pack played, and men of dubious reputation gathered to wind down from a tough winter of shakedowns, racketeering, and extortion.

But that development far up Collins Avenue was nothing compared to what was brewing at the end of that decade in Miami's island neighbor to the south. While Florida and especially Key West had always been a haven for the occasional Cuban exile and dissident, the residents of Miami had no idea how significantly a bearded ex-attorney named Fidel Castro was about to change their lives. With apologies to James W. Hall, it was the events of the 1959 Cuban Revolution that were to change the nature of the "American Riviera" forevermore, and to set the stage for Miami's emergence as the City of the Twenty-First Century.

With Batista overthrown, and Cuba's banks, farms and industries nationalized under a Communist-influenced regime, some 150,000 refugees fled to South Florida between 1959 and 1962, many of them members of the middle- and upper-classes. These Cubans brought with them money, political savvy, moral outrage and a vision uncharacteristic of the "typical" immigrant community. The influx was to transform the region instantaneously, creating not just a significant Hispanic populace, but a bicultural force that has only grown steadily since.

Grand Illusion  *Collins Avenue*

Federal Courthouse *Downtown*

Cuban immigration reached a peak of sorts, in 1980, when Castro emptied his prisons and simultaneously relaxed Cuban emigration policies. The resulting influx, known as the Mariel Boatlift, brought some 100,000 Cubans to South Florida in a matter of weeks, straining schools, public assistance agencies, law enforcement, and the entire social infrastructure of the region to the maximum. And yet, as it traditionally has, Miami met the challenge.

Economic hardship and political upheaval abroad were to encourage succeeding waves of immigration from nearly every nation in the Caribbean, Central and South America. Officials estimated that of the roughly two million people living in Dade County in 1995, more than fifty-five percent were Hispanic. Schools, public services agencies and local governments routinely carry on business in bilingual fashion.

The period of transition from 1959 through the late 80's — let's call it "During Miami Vice," anyway — has not always been tranquil, of course. Crime rates rose markedly, affecting not only the disadvantaged but at times spilling over into the tourist community and spawning headlines worldwide. While the same tragic events might take place a hundred times over in other modern cities over the course of a day, it is something else again when senseless tragedy strikes in paradise — the mind simply rebels at the contrast between such actions and the promise and beauty of the backdrop. Likewise, Miami's location, while exotic, also made it a nat-

Glory *Downtown*

ural point of entry for drug-runners, spanning the hit television series of the 80's. And political intrigue and conflict has been rife. From the ill-fated Bay of Pigs invasion, when some 1,500 Cuban patriots attempted to re-take their homeland, and the subsequent Cuban Missile Crisis, to the trial and subsequent imprisonment of Panamanian Manuel Noriega on drug-related charges, Miami long has been at the focal point of relations between North and South America.

Freedom Tower *Downtown*

Freedom Tower Up Close

For some long-time Miami residents, it was all too much to take. "White Flight," the resulting migration northward to Broward and Palm Beach counties, ensued. Disgruntled, change-resistant residents sported a popular bumper sticker in the 1980's: "Will The Last American Leaving Miami Please Take The Flag." And when Hurricane Andrew, the most costly in United States history, roared in from Africa in 1992, virtually leveling the southern half of Dade County, there were many who wondered if a death-knell hadn't been sounded.

But as always in Miami history, the skeptics have been proven wrong. While the process of rebuilding South Dade was a gargantuan task that still continues in some pockets, visitors once again travel tree-lined boulevards that lead to a rebuilt Metro-Zoo, to a newly-opened Homestead Motor Sports Complex where NASCAR races are held, to malls and shops and restaurants and golf courses and a myriad of tourist attractions that were utterly obliterated by the storm, now risen and shining once again.

If anything, the devastation of Andrew, which might have torn an already strained social fabric completely asunder, seems to have had the opposite effect on residents of Greater Miami. "We have come through

Citizen Swearing in Ceremony

this together," is the operative explanation for this new spirit of togetherness. A new district-based electoral process for choosing county commissioners gives voice to local concerns in the cumbersome process of governing a population of 2,000,000 spread across the largest urban area in the U.S. A series of incorporation movements for new villages within the county — Key Biscayne, Pinecrest, Aventura — aims at addressing similar issues. The Beacon Council, Dade's chief agency for the encouragement of industrial development, reports that 76,000 new jobs have been created since 1991 and that single-family home sales in the area impacted most severely by the hurricane more than doubled in the years that followed. The Greater Miami Convention and Visitors Bureau reported that tourism, including foreign tourism, had risen to 9.4 million in 1995, an all-time high, and by the first quarter of 1996 had climbed yet another 7.5 percent.

New Citizens Celebrate *Miami Convention Center*

Rehearsal / Miami City Ballet  *Miami Beach*

Miami continues to grow and to mature as a community, where newcomers can find not only a foothold but a cultural haven as well. The town that became known for fast cars and flashy clothes in the early 80's today hosts the Miami Book Fair, a week-long extravaganza of writers and writing that takes over a major portion of the downtown area and has become the largest of its kind. The New World School of the Arts (Miami's "Fame Academy") attracts high school student-artists nationwide, as do Master of Fine Arts programs in creative writing and the other arts at Florida International University and the University of Miami. Miami City Ballet, The Greater Miami Opera, The New World Symphony Orchestra, The Miami Film Festival and The Coconut Grove Playhouse all enjoy national reputations as venues in their respective arts, each reflecting in programming and personnel the distinctive cultural pluralism of Miami. There is a vital local theater network and a vast community of local artists which finds its apotheosis in the Coconut Grove Arts Festival, among the many other open-air festivals held throughout the year.

While rafters still brave the waters separating Cuba and Haiti from South Florida, while an often-fractious government wrangles over this approach and that, while social servants and civic leaders struggle to find the funds for over-burdened schools and public assistance agencies, Miami not only endures, but grows. Each new group enriches the existing tapestry, each conflict and each tragedy only strengthens the communal resolve. For Miami is a physical paradise, to be sure, and it houses a treasure-trove of riches created by its inhabitants. No one who's been here long enough to fill up a pair of shoes with sand can mistake that. And for the millions who have stayed, they are reminded each day: this is no made-up city, no mere playground, no simple land of the lotus-eaters, but a living laboratory of promise, a place where dreams begin, where, with work and determination, they can and do come true.

Looking In  *Miami City Ballet*

DeSoto Fountain  *Coral Gables*

Architectural Details  *DeSoto Fountain*

Douglas Entrance  *Coral Gables*

Coral Gables                                                                Star Fruit Tree *Coral Gables*

Alhambra Water Tower  *Coral Gables*

Alhambra Water Tower

Music Room *Vizcaya*

Ceiling / Music Room  *Vizcaya*

Coral Gables City Hall

Coral Gables City Hall

Holocaust Museum *Miami Beach*

Anguish  *Holocaust Museum*

Flashback *South Beach*

Togetherness

Peaceful Encounter *Liberty City*

Community Pride

Ukrainian Catholic Church  *Red Road*

Ukrainian Catholic Church

Spectator Sport / Domino Park  *Little Havana*

Culture and Tradition  *Domino Park*

Profile of Tradition *Little Havana*

Literally a Tradition *Collins Avenue*

Fruits of Labor  *Calle Ocho*

Calling it a Day  *Calle Ocho*

Delegates of Delight  *Miami Book Fair International*

Miami Book Fair International                    Dade County Youth Fair

Coconut Grove Arts Festival

Coming Together *Coconut Grove Arts Festival*

Colors of Bayside                                                    Miami Book Fair International

Art in Public Places  *Downtown*

Stepping into History  *Little Havana*

Centennial Celebration  *Bayfront Park*

Classic on Collins

# Deco

No other term is as evocative of the style of South Beach or SoBe, as the hot, hot, hot lower tip of the former barrier island and cattle ranch has come to be known. Where in the 40's and 50's families on a budget once congregated, where in the 60's and 70's oldsters later gathered, elbow to elbow on broad terrazzo porches, their white nose shades all pointed out toward the swells of the Atlantic like the beaks of strange shore birds, now throngs of the hip and watchers-of-the-hip nightly jam a dozen blocks of sea front promenade that is home to more chi-chi restaurants, shops, sidewalk cafes, and retro hotels and condominiums than anywhere else on earth...in the Deco style, that is.

The new denizens of SoBe are drawn by the proximity to the beach, to the breezes, to the breakers, and by the desire to be where the action is, of course, but consciously or not, they are also drawn, as have been all the populations before them, by the fanciful nature of the backdrop against which they play, the densest, most extensive collection of Art Deco architecture extant.

The French brought Art Deco to the attention of the world in the mid-1920's. Moderne, as it is also known, refers more to a mode of decoration than an actual architectural style, a playful, sleek-surfaced approach that favors glass, plastic, and shaped concrete in designs that evoke machines and the promise of technology in everything from mass-produced stemware and living room furniture to hotel lobbies and building facades. The style implied a certain faith in man's ability to control his environment, and in the very notion of progress itself, not an unattractive concept for a world populace reeling from the effects of the Great Depression. For whatever reasons, Deco flourished in the late 20's and 30's, and became the signature style in boom towns everywhere: Paris, yes, but also Tulsa, Minneapolis, Cleveland, and, of course, Miami Beach.

South Beach

Deco Style *Bal Harbour*

The 1940's ushered in a different set of concerns worldwide, and the Deco movement faded away, to be replaced by the sober, no-nonsense styles that have dominated the design of public building ever since...but Deco has remained alive and well in South Florida. The hotels and the apartment buildings done up Deco during the building craze of the 20's and 30's transformed themselves into modest accommodations for families, then to havens for retirees. By the end of the 1970's, some were pressed into service, housing Mariel refugees, and many more were falling before the wrecking ball, making way for parking lots and bigger, more streamlined, more functional — ie, soulless — apartment buildings, shops, and lodgings.

Which is where Barbara Capitman came in. Captiman, founder of the Miami Design Preservation League, is generally credited as the savior of the now world-famous Art Deco District on Miami Beach. Her fervor for the hundreds of pastel-accented buildings on the south end of the island led to the formation of the Art Deco Festival in the late 1970's, one of the first such celebrations of the style, an event that has grown to attract thousands of visitors from South Florida and around the world each year.

Miami Beach

Miami bookseller Mitchell Kaplan, whose shop Books & Books has been a significant supporter of the Deco Fair from the beginning, remembers growing up on Miami Beach, surrounded by Deco artifacts: "It was hard to take things too seriously surrounded by such a gathering of fantastic shapes and surfaces," he says. "This was the 1960's after all, and as a politically conscious young man, I remember feeling a little jealous of people who got to live in sober-looking cities like Boston and Berkeley and Chicago where it seemed more likely that free speech and civil rights movements would be taken seriously."

Kaplan says it with a smile, but he's a native, and an astute observer of the local scene. "Miami Beach has always been sold as a kind of fantasy destination," he says, "and Deco is the perfect reflection of that concept. In many ways, the world has come around to a fascination with style over substance, so it's not so surprising that Deco should enjoy this renaissance."

Maybe the world has changed. But Kaplan offers one more explanation for this singularly captivating blend of place and style, perhaps the most intriguing of all: "Deco style seems ship-like in a lot of ways, you know, all the curves and graceful lines. Sometimes I think it's as if the whole city is poised there by the water, ready to set sail."

Quite a fantasy, all right. But doesn't it seem appropriate somehow: an entire city on the continent's glittery edge, ready for a voyage to the future and all those dreams out ahead.

Color Coordinated *Miami Beach*

Collins Avenue                                                    Ocean Drive

Nightlight  *South Beach*

Art Deco Weekend *South Beach*

Henry Sax  *Brickell Avenue*                    Dancin' in the Street  *Ocean Drive*

Reflecting on the Past *Ocean Drive*

Park Central *Ocean Drive*

Net Worth  *South Beach*

Ocean Drive

Deco Detail I / Ceiling Berkeley Shore Hotel

Deco Detail II / Ceiling  *Berkeley Shore Hotel*

South Beach

Deco Lifeguard Stand  *South Beach*

Beach Patrol Building *Ocean Drive*

Deco by Design

Deco Bus Stop  *Collins Avenue*

Just Coincidence?  *Miami Beach*

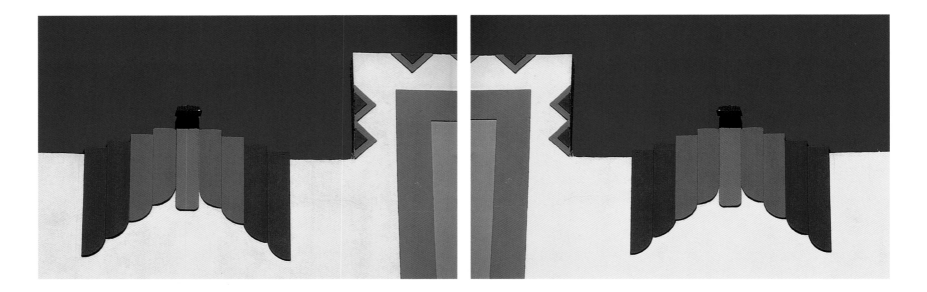

Thunderbirds *Ocean Drive*

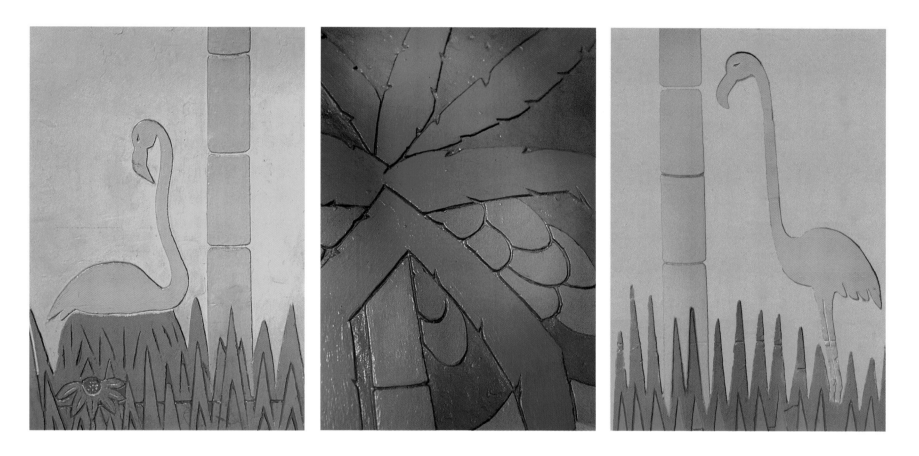

Flamingo Plaza  *Miami Beach*

The Gallery  *Ocean Drive*

The Gallery In Part

The Delano & The National  *Collins Avenue*

Mirage / Ritz Plaza  *Collins Avenue*

Magic Hour  *View from Star Island*

# The Light

"It's the light that's so special here," says poet and Nobel Laureate Derek Walcott, waving his arm at the panorama before him.  Walcott, a native of the tiny Caribbean nation of St. Lucia, stands on a fourth-floor balcony that overlooks a glittering hook of Biscayne Bay.  Far across the water a phalanx of condominium buildings and hotels marches down the horizon, marking the northern end of Miami Beach.  It's evening, and the sun has sunk behind the feathery Australian pines at Walcott's back, but the distant buildings are tall enough to catch the last glow from the sky.  The pale buildings have turned roseate, the sky is milk, the water a cobalt blue that's rapidly shading to steel.  "Good Lord, man," says Walcott.  "It makes me want to paint."

Local Artist Adrienne Goyette  *Coral Gables*

"I came to Miami from Ithaca, New York," says artist Sandy Winter, "and I was immediately struck by how much more constant and intense the light was here. For most artists, intense light changes your sense of color, intensifies it, but I thought I was pretty well set in my ways. I remember a local gallery owner telling me, 'We'll see how Miami changes your sense of color,' and I thought to myself, nobody messes with my color." Winter laughs. "You can't escape the light here, though. My colors became so much brighter, yellower, richer. There's a vibrancy in Latin art that I love and that I was surprised and pleased to see coming into my work."

Winter pauses, then turns to the essence of the matter: "There's an intensity and clarity to the light that you don't get anywhere else, sure, but that's not all there is to it. One of my first reactions to Miami concerned the amazing contradictions that you get here: even when you see something slightly seedy or possibly sinister, you find it juxtaposed against the beauty of the physical landscape and the openness of the clean, clear light. It creates an unspoken tension, a sense that what's not being said is as important as what's more obvious in a work. That's the important thing I strive for in my painting; Miami's not just about being pretty, sunsets and seascapes and so on. It's much richer than that."

Bougainvillea *Coral Gables*

173

Urban Highlights

Pulse of the City

Moonrise *Port of Miami*

Overview *Downtown*

Enchanted Evening *Coral Gables*

Graphic by Nature  *Coral Gables*

The Light  *Card Sound Road*

Edge of Darkness  *Card Sound Bridge*

Tropical Enlightenment  *Coral Gables*

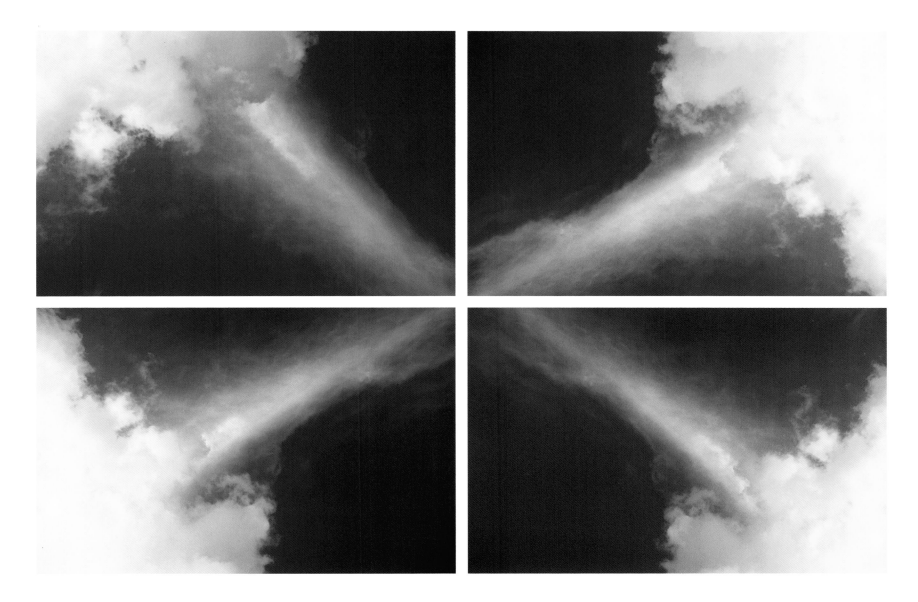

Cloud Four-Mation

Just in Passing *Calle Ocho*

Hot Lips/Moth Orchid  *Fairchild Gardens*

Fairchild Gardens

Fairchild Gardens

Positive Outlook  *Coral Gables*

Morning Light  *Ocean Drive*

Reflecting  *Ocean Drive*

The Camillus House
Hope for All Mural
was conceived & painted
by Miami artist César Augusto.

It was inspired by
Shelly Dreer
of Camillus Health Concern

This mural is dedicated
to homeless people
everywhere.
November 22, 1992

César
Augusto

Compassion  *Camillus House*

Shade and Shadows *Coral Gables*

Branching Out / Banyan Tree *Coral Gables*

Slice of Life *Ocean Drive*

Dog's Life  *Ocean Drive*

Into the Horizon *MacArthur Causeway*

Setting Sun  *MacArthur Causeway*

Light and life in Miami.

# Commentary

By Sharon L. Wells, Historian

*The following pages provide additional information about many images in this book and are listed in order of first appearance. Locations on page 203 appear alphabetically.*

**PAGE 8, 86, 87, 88, 89**
**ORANGE BOWL**
In the very first Orange Bowl game, held in 1933 in a wooden stadium, the University of Miami defeated Manhattan College. Thus commenced the marvelous annual parade and festivities. The 74,000-seat Orange Bowl stadium continued to host a crucial post-season bowl game— in 1984, the Miami Hurricanes defeated the Nebraska Cornhuskers. In the 1995 finale at the Orange Bowl field, Florida State defeated Notre Dame, 31-26, closing the book on a momentous chapter of college gridiron history. Future Orange Bowl games will be played at Pro Player Park (formerly Joe Robbie Stadium).

**PAGE 10, 120, 121**
**HOLOCAUST MUSEUM**
1933-1945 Meridian Avenue
A huge, bronze outstretched hand, " the sculpture of love and anguish," sits within a tranquil reflecting pool that is edged by Jerusalem stone from Israel. These archetypal elements combine to form sculptor Kenneth Treister's gripping tribute to the memory of six million Jews, victims of the Nazi atrocities during World War II. Five years in the creation, the public meditation gardens were commissioned by the local Holocaust Memorial Committee in April, 1985. The City of Miami Beach donated public lands for the site. According to its creator, the hand exemplifies "the final reaching out of a dying person." The 130 life-size figures that cling to the hand, representing the anguish of death, were cast in bronze by 45 Mexican craftsmen. The garden statuary, internationally acclaimed, honors both the Jewish culture irrevocably lost and the presence of Miami Beach's survivor Jewish population.

**PAGE 11**
**CORAL CASTLE**
28655 South Dixie Highway
Edward Leedskalnin, an eccentric from Metei, Latvia, five feet tall and weighing just ninety-seven pounds, applied a unique system of jacks, wedges, cables and pulleys, and a knowledge of weights and leverage, to construct a 3-acre coral limestone folk environment. Working alone from 1920 to 1940, Leedskalnin, with little formal education but an obsession for science and astronomy, quarried slabs of native rock for his edifice. The wondrous complex includes a 23-ton monolith of a crescent moon and 18-ton sculptures of Mars and Saturn. Legend has it that the tiny Latvian built his Rock Castle as a tribute to "Sweet Sixteen" Agnes Scuff, a 16-year old who spurned his love. The creator was also a tour guide, charging visitors 25 cents. Leedskalnin died in 1951 and left no will. In 1953 Julius Levin purchased the property through probate, and re-named it Coral Castle. He opened this fantastic architectural oddity as a tourist attraction. Placed on the National Register of Historic Places in 1984, Coral Castle is a truly unique monument to Leedskalnin's infinite patience, his enduring passions, astronomic and engineering experimentation, and his lost love.

**PAGE 12, 135B**
**DADE COUNTY YOUTH FAIR**
The Dade County Youth Fair, initiated in 1952, began as a showcase for 4-H students. Today the 18-day exposition is set in a permanent fair facility that showcases over 40,000 student and adult award-winning exhibits and is recognized as one of North America's premier fairs and expositions.

**PAGE 13, 124**
**MARTIN LUTHER KING MURAL**
Liberty City
The vast wall mural in Liberty City, painted by Oscar Thomas, memorializes Dr. King, who appeared here on April 14, 1966, to observe the founding of Miami's chapter of the Southern Christian Leadership Conference, declaring, " I still have a dream, a dream of one nation."

**PAGE 14**
**MUSEUM OF CONTEMPORARY ART**
770 N. E. 125th Street, North Miami
Art and architecture merged dramatically with the February, 1996, opening of the Museum of Contemporary Art's glittering new work space. Architect Charles Gwathmey described it as "a building reminiscent of a Cubist collage in color and structure. It is both experimental and provocative, enriching the dialogue between art and architecture." The museum, founded in 1981, initiated its permanent collection, including masterworks by artists such as Robert Rauschenberg, Larry Rivers, Agnes Martin and Jasper Johns, in 1995. Jack Pierson's neon sign fixtures, PARADISE, 1995, are displayed at the Museum of Contemporary Art. The work is courtesy of Track 16 Gallery, Santa Monica; Luhring Augustine, New York; Richard Kuhlenschmit and the artist. The installation in Miami was sponsored by Portofino Tower.

**PAGE 15**
**EVERGLADES**
The Everglades, a national preserve of primeval swamplands, is a unique kingdom. A natural landscape, exotic and rich with wildlife, the Everglades represents an ecosystem unequaled in the world. Over a million and a quarter acres contain marshlands, cypress swamps, towering hardwood hammocks, seas of saw grass, and watery mangroves that teem with an infinite variety of birds, plants and animals. Named the "Pa-ha-okee" (grass river) by Indians, the immense acreage was dedicated as Everglades National Park in 1947 by President Harry Truman. Declared a World Heritage Site by UNESCO in 1982, the national park offers visitors a splendid glimpse of nature unrefined.

**PAGE 18**
**MARJORY STONEMAN DOUGLAS**
Arriving in 1915 from Massachusetts, Marjory Stoneman Douglas, Coconut Grove's most distinguished citizen, celebrated her 106th birthday in 1996. Douglas penned the 1947 classic, The Everglades: River of Grass , a literary masterpiece, eloquently evoking the fragility of that extraordinary and vast resource. Its publication led to the designation of Everglades National Park that same year. As a journalist, a crusader for women's rights, and an author, Douglas is peerless—inspiring two generations of environmentalists for fifty years. She remains a remarkable, and indomitable, champion of causes close to her heart.

**PAGE 19**
**FLORIDA PANTHER**
The Florida panther, one of the rarest animals on earth, was placed on the Endangered Species list in 1967. The panther (Felis concolor coryl), now confined to certain sections of the Florida Everglades, is designated as the official mammal of Florida, though only approximately 30-50 remain in the wild.

**PAGE 20**
**AMERICAN ALLIGATOR**
For decades a popular Florida motif, the alligator, North America's largest reptile, shares a common ancestor with dinosaurs. Although placed on the endangered list in 1967, the alligator mississipiensis is making a comeback, but remains a threatened species today. Its round snout and unexposed fourth tooth differentiate it from the crocodile. Gators have also become part of Florida's lifestyle—sometimes frequenting golf courses, gardens, hotel lobbies, drains or canals.

**PAGE 22, 23**
**TOMATOES**
The growth of winter vegetables on the farmlands of South Florida, a key sector of America's agriculture, provides a significant cash crop. Dade County is still the winter capital for the harvesting of red, juicy tomatoes in the United States.

**PAGE 28A**
**MIAMI INTERNATIONAL AIRPORT**
America's second busiest hub for international travelers, Miami International Airport was dubbed America's Gateway to the Americas in 1928. Home to world famous aviators such as Glenn Curtiss and Capt. Eddie Rickenbacker, the World War I flying ace who later headed Eastern Airlines, MIA dedicated its new passenger terminal in 1959. Jumbo jet service was inaugurated at this site of the original Pan American Airfield in October, 1970.

**PAGE 29A**
**MIAMI RIVER**
From the air, metropolitan Miami sprawls towards Biscayne Bay. At the turn of the century, Miami's residents numbered but 5,000. Today the population totals over two million. First came the Tequesta Indians, followed by the Spaniards' discovery of the Miami estuary in the sixteenth century. Then the Bahamian wreckers, and still later the Seminole Indians arrived in the 1830's. Ft. Dallas, an Army garrison, was built on the north bank of Miami River in 1837, and abandoned in 1842. In 1844 the county seat was moved to the "Miami River where it empties into Biscaino Bay." Settlers arrived, but it was only after the Civil War that the pioneer village of Miami began to take root. The river itself runs westward, becoming Miami Canal, and eventually Lake Okeechobee; to the south, Miami River, a major commercial waterway for cargo, terminates in downtown Miami.

**PAGE 29B**
**BICYCLES TO HAITI**
Bound for Haiti and the Caribbean, salvaged bicycles are collected for disbursement to the Third World.

**PAGE 37**
**FIRST UNION TOWER**
201 Biscayne Boulevard
The distinctive First Union Tower, Florida's tallest structure, rises 55 stories, and includes 1.2 million square feet of interior space. Plans were drawn in 1984 by Charles E. Bassett and Skidmore, Owens & Merrill. Its presence is transcendent at nightfall.

**PAGE 41**
**VIZCAYA BREAKWATER AND STATUARY**
Deering called his estate "Vizcaya" after the Spanish province of the same name that lies next to the Bay of Biscay. The Great Stone Barge was designed as a breakwater, creating safe harbor for visiting vessels and sailing craft that docked at Vizcaya. Aboard the Great Stone Barge are "the delights and terrors of the sea," statuary figures by sculptor A. Stirling Calder. The eastern elevation of Villa Vizcaya overlooks Miami's Biscayne Bay. Above the balcony to Mr. Deering's personal bedroom is a sundial inscribed with the Latin words for "Accept the gifts of the hour joyfully and relinquish them stoically." A seahorse weathervane adorns the palazzo's crest.

**PAGE 42, 49**
**STILTSVILLE**
Among the flats of Biscayne Bay, a mile south of Cape Florida Lighthouse, the last remnants of Stiltsville are still visible. A community of propped up homes, rustic houses and falling down wrecks, Stiltsville is rapidly disappearing—a victim of environmental concerns. A decades-old getaway for liveaboards,

Stiltsville became part of Biscayne National Park in 1980. Rustic saloons and gambling floats like the 1939 Quarterback Club, Crawfish Eddie's and Plucky Pierre's Bikini Club, busted in 1965, are but legend. Established prior to 1937, Stiltsville included 12 shacks and two clubs by 1945. By 1999, these picturesque retreats will exist only as memories.

**PAGE 44**
**GOVERNMENT CUT AND SOUTH POINTE**
Led by Miami Mayor John Sewall, the U. S. Government was persuaded in 1905 to dredge a 500-foot wide cut at the south end of Miami Beach, allowing the bay and the ocean to merge. This deepened the harbor, improved access to the port of Miami, and created Fisher Island. South Pointe, once the location of the Miami Beach Kennel Club, is presently a prime urban development site where high-rise condominiums will forever alter the vista at Miami Beach's tip.

**PAGE 52**
**VIZCAYA FROG & LIZARD FOUNTAIN**
Vizcaya's fan-shaped gardens are uniquely glorious, arrayed with Italian-clipped topiary, stone statuary, balustrades, grottos, waterways and vine-clad gazebos. Drawing upon historic Italian hill garden concepts, Colombian-born Diego Suarez, trained in Florence's Accademia dei Belle Arti, blended Europe's traditional garden techniques with South Florida's sub-tropical plant materials. Carved lead figures of frogs and lizards, designed by Charles Cary Rumsey, decorate the sarcophagus-shaped fountain basin, which sits prominently on the South Terrace of Villa Vizcaya.

**PAGE 56**
**DINNER KEY**
In 1917, at the opening of World War I, a U. S. Navy seaplane base and training school opened on this spit of dredged land.

**PAGE 57**
**DINNER KEY MARINA**
This small island off Coconut Grove has been transformed into Miami's largest marina, hosting nine piers and 581 boat moorings. The marina offers a truly scenic panoramic vista, with pelicans perched like statues or diving for dinner.

**PAGE 58, 176**
**PORT OF MIAMI**
This world famous seaport, situated on two man-made keys, Dodge Island and Lummus Island, opened in June, 1965. The Port of Miami has emerged as the largest cruise ship port in the world, a first class gateway for over three million passengers to Latin America and the Caribbean each year.

**PAGE 67**
**PLANET HOLLYWOOD**
3390 Mary Street, Coconut Grove
Hollywood stars glamorized The Grove at Planet Hollywood's opening bash in May, 1994. The all-star spectacle included owners Sylvester Stallone (a recent Coconut Grove homeowner), Bruce Willis, Demi Moore and Arnold Schwarzenegger. The flash and glitz restaurant continues to be a popular, memorabilia-filled dining experience.

**PAGE 68, 131**
**WOLFIE'S**
2038 Collins Avenue
Wolfie's, the Miami Beach landmark eatery, is always crowded, and open twenty-four hours a day. Restauranteur "Wolfie" Cohen, called the "million dollar rascal," originated Wolfie's back in 1947. Cohen held a public contest to name his restaurant. The prize? Free meals for a year. Eight people submitted the name "Wolfie's," and all eight winners dined for one year — free. Since then, the popular delicatessen has served up millions of cheese blintzes, bagels, matzoh balls, and bowls of sauerkraut, along with a tradition steeped in nostalgia. Although hot kosher corned beef sandwiches no longer cost 60 cents, diners have their favorite foods and favorite waitresses still. Joe Nevel, the present owner, first ate at Wolfie's in 1948 and finally purchased it in 1984.

**PAGE 77**
**EXOTIC WILDLIFE RESCUE TEAM**
All critters, natives and exotics, are the domain of Todd Hartwick's 15-year old private wildlife control group, Pesky Critters. Hartwick views each day as an urban safari, capturing orphaned or injured animals. Any species sporting fin, fur or feathers—from wild cockatoos to lost boa constrictors—may become the focus of a day's efforts.

**PAGE 78**
**HURRICANE ANDREW**
On August 24, 1992, Hurricane Andrew struck. A Category Four powerhouse, with winds up to 130 miles per hour, Andrew tore in from Cape Verde off the African coast. Battering South Florida relentlessly, it ultimately claimed 24 victims, proving to be the costliest natural disaster in American history. Over 200,000 people were left homeless, neighborhoods were destroyed, native vegetation was uprooted and obliterated. The U. S. armed forces set up temporary quarters for the homeless in tent cities, an experience at once harrowing and profound. Recovery has brought stricter building codes and a renewed spirit of community.

**PAGE 80, 81**
**HIALEAH PARK**
2200 East 4th Avenue
The Grand Dame for thoroughbred racing, Hialeah Park is the oldest existing recreational facility of its kind in South Florida. In 1925 aviator Glenn Curtiss and cattleman James Bright created the park —- its racetracks, stables, infield turf track, jai-lai fronton, amusement park festooned with a roller coaster and Chief Willy Willy's Miccosukee Indian Village. Philadelphian Joseph H. Widener purchased the park after portions were destroyed by the 1926 hurricane. Enhancing his 206-acre site, Widener constructed a new walking rink, patterned after one at Longchamps, France. The 1953 Mediterranean Revival-influenced clubhouse and the magnificent grandstand, together with the meticulous grounds, lakes, gardens and tracks, are listed on the National Register of Historic Places. The nation's largest domestic flock of pink flamingos, descendants of those imported from Cuba, dwell at Hialeah Park.

**PAGE 83**
**DON SHULA**
Don Shula, the Miami Dolphins' legendary head coach from 1969 to 1995, led his team to a perfect season (17-0) in 1972-73—an incredible winning streak never duplicated. Shula is the winningest coach in football history, with 318 NFL victories. Until he retired in 1995, Shula was the Dolphins' first and only coach. Voted the Coach of the Decade in 1980 by the Pro Football Hall of Fame, Shula adopted as his motto: "Success is never final; defeat is never fatal."

**PAGE 85**
**DAN MARINO**
Currently the star quarterback for the Miami Dolphins, Dan Marino won two AFC championships in 1983 and 1985, playing in two Super Bowls. Born in 1961, Marino, a standout at the University of Pittsburgh, was selected the NFL's Rookie of the Year in 1981. He holds the NFL career record for most games (10) with 400 or more yards passing; most seasons (5) with 4,000 or more yards passing; most seasons (9) with 3,000 or more yards passing. Marino was voted the NFL's Most Valuable Player for 1984-85 and continues his illustrious career as starting quarterback for the Miami Dolphins.

**PAGE 90**
**VILLA VIZCAYA**
3251 South Miami Avenue
In 1914 James Deering, the wealthy vice-president of International Harvester and an inveterate art collector, commissioned architect F. Burrall Hoffman, Jr., of New York's Carrere and Hastings, to create a winter resort set amid the native hardwood hammock facing Biscayne Bay. From 1914 to 1917, Hoffman crafted Villa Vizcaya, a fabulous 76-room palazzo, employing 1,000 workers (one-tenth of Miami's population). The design, a central courtyard opening to arcades and loggias, was adapted to the local climate. Vizcaya, modeled after the Villa Rezzonico near Venice, is the first, and finest, example of Italian Renaissance architecture in America. Deering's decorator, Paul Chalfin, former curator at Boston's Museum of Fine Arts, traveled throughout Europe selecting objects, tapestries, fine antiques and furniture, including Catherine de Medici's 16th century fireplace, to furnish Vizcaya. Grandeur, extravagance and splendor define this present-day museum of decorative arts. Deering wintered at Vizcaya every year until he died at sea aboard a French liner in 1925. His heirs sold the property to Dade County in 1952 for one million dollars. Deering's legacy lives on. Vizcaya, now a museum, is open to the public.

**PAGE 92**
**CAPE FLORIDA LIGHTHOUSE**
The Cape Florida Lighthouse, a crucial link in a series of seacoast navigational aids, was completed in 1825. Located at the tip of the barrier island of Key Biscayne, the sentinel assisted seafarers trafficking along Florida's precarious coastal reefs. The 65-foot tower was destroyed during a Seminole Indian raid on July 23, 1836. When rebuilding was authorized a year later, contractors discovered a fraud perpetrated by the original builder. Hollow bricks had been used! A solid red brick tower was re-constructed by 1846 and its height raised to 95 feet in 1855. At Miami's Centennial celebration in July, 1996, the newly restored Cape Florida Lighthouse's lantern was re-lighted. Today this National Register property stands as a signal landmark within the surrounding Bill Baggs Cape Florida State Park.

**PAGE 94, 95**
**VENETIAN POOL**
2701 DeSoto Boulevard
The European influence that defines Coral Gables' architecture also touched the masterful, Venice-inspired municipal swimming pool. Limestone croppings create diving platforms amid the lush, natural lagoon and falling water cascades over rock formations. Striped Venetian lamp posts adorn the waterscape, and gondolas once linked the pool to Biscayne Bay. Famed orator William Jennings Bryan extolled the virtues of Coral Gables as part of George Merrick's expansive real estate sales campaign in the Twenties. Originally built atop a rock quarry site in 1924, the open air pool was fed by artesian well water. A $2.3 million restoration in 1989 led to listing on the National Register of Historic Places.

**PAGE 97**
**GEORGE MERRICK HOUSE**
907 Coral Way
Reverend Solomon Merrick, emigrating from New England, homesteaded 160 acres in South Florida, planted grapefruit orchards and began constructing his family's domicile in 1898. Merrick chose oolitic limestone rock, quarried by Bahamian laborers, and native Dade County pine timbers as his building materials. Its classic simplicity is marked by a coral tile gable roof and prominent second story Palladian window. The elder Merrick called his home "Coral Gables" after Grover Cleveland's Grey

Gables in Massachusetts. Later his son George adopted the name of his boyhood home for the stylish city he fashioned in the 1920's. Merrick himself fell victim to the real estate bust. He operated a Florida Keys fishing camp until it was destroyed in the 1935 hurricane, and later was appointed Postmaster of Miami. George Merrick died at age fifty-six in 1942.

**PAGE 98**
**BILTMORE HOTEL**
1200 Anastasia Avenue
The Biltmore Hotel looms as the flagship building of Coral Gables. Moorish in design and sienna in color, the opulent Biltmore was erected between 1925-26 by Leonard Schultze and S. Fullerton Weaver, architects for New York's Waldorf Astoria and The Breakers in Palm Beach. The Biltmore even ran special passenger trains from New York to service what was called "the last word in the evolution of civilisation, the acme of hostelry and clubs." This premier resort, filled with Italian marble and Tiffany china, was abandoned and served as a hospital during World War II. Today the 26-story tower, a replica of Seville's Giralda Tower, stands as the centerpiece of a magnificent $52 million restoration completed in 1985. Owned by the City of Coral Gables, the Biltmore re-opened under a long term lease in 1992. And the huge pool, with a capacity of 1,250,000 gallons of water, was once the site where swimming instructor Johnny Weissmuller broke world records.

**PAGE 99**
**EVERGLADES SUITE, BILTMORE**
The elaborate Everglades Suite is the only 2-story space in the Biltmore Hotel's magnificent tower and contains a mezzanine level. For a time it served as Coral Gables' founder George Merrick's personal office. Luminaries such as the Duke and Duchess of Windsor once enjoyed overnight stays in the deluxe suite. The gold leaf ceiling decorations, with intricately painted scenes of tropical Florida, and the crystal chandeliers are original.

**PAGE 100**
**PLAZA de la CUBANIDAD**
Jose Marti, Cuba's honored martyr who led the 1890's revolutionary war for independence, is memorialized at this patriots' monument in Little Havana. A quote from Marti, "Las palmas son novias que esperan" ("The palm trees are girlfriends who wait"), is inscribed near the fountain. It has been dedicated as a place of hope for a quarter million Cuban refugees, newly arrived residents of Miami.

**PAGE 101**
**FONTAINEBLEAU MURAL**
4441 Collins Avenue
Morris Lapidus' monumental Fontainebleau Hotel, described in his autobiography, Architecture of Joy, as "an exuberance in motion," becomes an extraordinary, fool-the-eye traffic stopper in Richard Haas' 13,000 square foot wall painting. The trompe l'oeil mural features an immense illusionist archway framing the undulating, white Fontainebleau set amid lush waterfalls— revealing to all what lies behind this fantastic wall.

**PAGE 102**
**U. S. FEDERAL COURTHOUSE**
300 N. E. First Avenue
The 1931-33 Post Office and Courthouse represents a finely crafted example of Spanish/Mediterranean Revival architecture. Dressed in grey coquina stone, the massive 3-story edifice is unusually elaborate for a federal structure. This present-day U. S. Courthouse is rectangular in plan, and topped by a hip roof covered with red mission tile. A 17-bay facade, articulated by Ionic pilasters and two engaged Corinthian columns, marks the restrained classical style. The top parapet is rich in details—intricately carved pelicans, flanking shields and a central eagle.

**PAGE 104, 105**
**FREEDOM TOWER**
600 Biscayne Boulevard
The Freedom Tower was erected originally as the home of the Miami Daily News, owned by James Cox, Democratic aspirant for president in 1920. Designed by Schultze & Weaver, architects for New York's Grand Central Station and Coral Gables' Biltmore Hotel, its striking tower, like the Biltmore's, was inspired by Seville's 13th century Giralda Tower. The landmark is Renaissance in style, yet Spanish baroque in detailing. A venerable monument, the 11-story Freedom Tower, erected in 1925, later served as the Cuban Refugee Center from 1962 to 1974. Placed on the National Register of Historic Places in 1979, this shrine of hope to Cuban emigres was abandoned for a decade, but lavishly restored in 1990.

**PAGE 106, 107**
**NEW CITIZENS BEING SWORN IN**
The demographics of South Florida changed dramatically in the 1980's. Miami, newly international, is the first metropolitan area in the United States with an Hispanic majority. The Mariel Boatlift of 1980 added 125,000 new emigres. Refugees from Nicaragua, Colombia, Haiti and Cuba have latinized the political, as well as social and cultural, life of Miami, lending credence to America's "melting pot" history.

**PAGE 108, 109**
**MIAMI CITY BALLET**
Miami City Ballet's storefront studio on South Beach's Lincoln Road Mall regularly draws passersby to watch rehearsals. The ten-year old company, which performs recitals nationally and internationally, was founded by artistic director Edward Villella.

**PAGE 110, 111**
**DESOTO FOUNTAIN**
Seville Avenue, Granada and DeSoto Boulevards
The graceful DeSoto Plaza, featuring the most imposing fountain in Coral Gables, was designed in 1925 by the ubiquitous Denman Fink. A significant civic monument, its embellishments include the pedestal fount, a beautiful central obelisk, ornate glass lanterns, and four faces carved in relief.

**PAGE 112**
**DOUGLAS ENTRANCE** (La Puerta del Sol )
Intersection of Douglas Road and S.W. 8th Street
George Merrick's urban design concept called for the placement of numerous Moorish style gateways, or portals, into "The City Beautiful." La Puerta del Sol, conceived as a 10-acre plaza with arcades and towers containing artists' studios and commercial space, was designed by architects Walter DeGarmo and Phineas Paist. In 1927 Douglas Entrance cost a million dollars, and was the fourth and last in a series of grand gateways constructed in Coral Gables. Contemporary adaptive re-use and recent restoration led to listing on the National Register of Historic Places.

**PAGE 113B**
**STAR FRUIT (CARAMBOLA)**
The star fruit, named for its designer-like shape when cut in cross-section, is native to Southeast Asia and Java. Typically used as a garnish, the colorful carambola lends beauty, texture and a citrus taste to gourmet plates. It is grown extensively in Florida, Hawaii and the Caribbean.

**PAGE 114, 115**
**ALHAMBRA WATER TOWER**
Intersection of Alhambra Circle, Greenway Court, and Ferdinand Street
Resembling a coastal lighthouse, the Alhambra Water Tower was designed by Denman Fink, Coral Gables' art director and George Merrick's uncle, in 1924. The tower was in use for only 6 years, then neglected for fifty. The tower with its intricate detailing, was faithfully restored, complete with copper dome, in 1993.

**PAGE 116, 117**
**VIZCAYA MUSIC ROOM & CHANDELIER**
Decorated in an Italian Rococo style, the Music Room's painted wall and ceiling panels once adorned a palace of Milan's Borromeo family. The musical instruments are antiques; and the harpsichord is signed and dated 1619 by its maker, Giovanni Battista Boni of Cortona, Italy.

**PAGE 118, 119**
**CORAL GABLES CITY HALL**
405 Biltmore Way
Beautifully ornate, the Mediterranean Revival city hall is the piece de resistance of architects Phineas Paist and Harold Steward. Its semi-circular facade is topped by twelve limestone columns, and the facing limestone is said to have been quarried in Key West. Financed by a $200,000 municipal bond, and opened in 1928, the building was modeled after William Strickland's nineteenth century Exchange Building in Philadelphia. The tri-tiered clock tower contains a 500 pound bell.

**PAGE 126, 127**
**ASSUMPTION UKRAINIAN CATHOLIC CHURCH**
58 N. W. 57th Avenue
The sparkling brass onion-dome of the Assumption Ukrainian Catholic Church lends a touch of the East to the multi-cultural ethnicity that defines Miami.

**PAGE 128, 129, 130**
**DOMINO PARK**
Along S.W. 15th Avenue, between Calle Ocho and Ninth Street, scenes reminiscent of old Havana still prevail. At Domino Park, older Cuban exiles, dressed in guayaberas (tropical white shirts), puffing cigars and drinking buches or cafe con leches, enjoy a traditional game of dominoes. In Little Havana, where Spanish remains the colloquial language, traditions endure.

**PAGE 134, 135A, 138B**
**MIAMI BOOK FAIR INTERNATIONAL**
For eight days in November the non-profit Miami Book Fair International stages an extraordinary literary event for over 500,000 bibliophiles. Readings and lectures by acclaimed authors, displays for over 300 national and international exhibitors, booths for rare book appraisals, writing workshops and literary performances highlight one of Miami's foremost cultural events.

**PAGE 136, 137**
**COCONUT GROVE ARTS FESTIVAL**
A record 1.2 million visitors enjoyed the 33rd Annual Coconut Grove Arts Festival in 1996. Conceived in 1963, the mid-February, 3-day juried festival sprawls for miles. Thousands of art gazers and collectors behold a panoramic display of paintings, watercolors, clay sculptures, photography, printmaking and drawing, jewelry and metal work, and glass objets d'art crafted by 326 artists from across the nation.

**PAGE 138A**
**BAYSIDE MARKETPLACE**
401 Biscayne Boulevard
Bayside, a marketplace created by Baltimore's Rouse Company ( who developed Boston's Faneuil Hall), is a downtown waterfront fixture. The shopping/entertainment complex, resembles a Caribbean straw market, with brightly colored buildings and tin-roof halls. Crowds of visiting cruise ship passengers, tourists, street performers and concert-goers frequent Bayside. Sparkling renovations to the 235,000 square feet of retail space in 1993 cost 11 million dollars.

**PAGE 139**
**SCULPTURE: DROPPED BOWL WITH SCATTERED SLICES AND PEELS**
Dade County adopted an Arts in Public Places ordinance in 1973, giving Metro-Dade County national visibility in the arts. By 1995, amid a cultural renaissance, over 450 works by regional and international artists—murals, sculptures, fountains, and environmental installations as well as small scale art works—had been placed. Artists Claes Oldenburg and Coosie van Bruggen's acclaimed sculpture, the inventive and colorful Dropped Bowl with Scattered Slices and Peels is a marvelous example of public art. The Dropped Bowl fountain presents an imaginary moment of contact when a bowl full of orange slices and peels drops onto the plaza at Government Center's park. The shape of the pools is a free version of the comic book "splat." Computerized water displays surround the eight cast concrete bowl fragments, weighing 124,000 pounds, four painted steel plate peels and five cast resin orange sections.

**PAGE 140, 141**
**MIAMI CENTENNIAL**
On July 28, 1996, Miami, "The Magic City," dressed up to celebrate its 100th birthday. The passage of a century saw the 1896 incorporation of the territory as a new city, the election of John B. Reilly as the first mayor, a population explosion from 1,681 residents in 1900 to a population of nearly two million in 1996 and the transformation of Julia Tuttle's original homestead into a thriving metropolis. With an early assist from Henry Flagler, Miami's palmetto scrub lands metamorphozed into the Land of Sunshine's tourist haven. Through boom and bust, the lure of Miami's land and climate triumphed.

**PAGE 142**
**MARLIN HOTEL**
1200 Collins Avenue
Inspired by the tropics and influenced by the Art Deco Style popularized at the 1925 Exposition Internationale des Arts Decoratifs et Industriels Modernes, hotelier David Levinson constructed the Marlin, the first of his landmark Deco hotels, in 1939. It thrived during the vacation heyday of the 50's when rooms rented for five to seven dollars a day. With its stepped parapet, rounded edges, and aquatic bas relief panels, the Marlin presents a spectacle of artistry.

**PAGE 148A, 156, 157**
**BERKELEY SHORE HOTEL**
1610 Collins Avenue
Architect Albert Anis dressed the Berkeley Shore's interior in curvilinear shapes and nautical motifs, punctuating the facade's stepped parapet with a towering "trylon," a decorative central needle-like mast. Completed in 1940, this premier example of tropical fantasy architecture retains the theatricality of a magical stage set. It's one of over 800 structures, set within a one square mile sector, that create Miami Beach's Deco District.

**PAGE 148B**
**CARDOZO HOTEL**
1300 Ocean Drive
Barbara Baer Capitman, the visionary who almost single-handedly rescued the Deco District's memorable hotels from demolition, saved the faded Cardozo Hotel, which became the first restoration along Ocean Drive in the early 1980's. In 1976 Capitman founded the Miami Design Preservation League and sparked the movement to preserve these magnificent, and unmatched, structures that embraced the flair of the Jazz Age, the art of Futurism and the fantasy of Surrealism. Capitman's worthy efforts helped create an enduring legacy—the establishment in 1979 of the first National Register Historic District of twentieth century landmarks. The Cardozo's original owner was Miami judge Benjamin Cardozo, later the eminent Supreme Court associate justice. Singer Gloria Estefan oversees its current chic incarnation.

**PAGE 149**
**PORTOFINO GROUP BUILDING**
Fifth Street, Miami Beach
The Portofino Group Building at South Beach's tip symbolizes the glass and glitz architecture of the new Miami. Dramatic lighting, constantly changing, casts the tower as a night-time chimera. Trendy China Grill, a celebrated New York restaurant, recently opened at this address.

**PAGE 150**
**ART DECO WEEK**
A favorite festival for Deco lovers, Art Deco Weekend, sponsored by Miami Design Preservation League, occurs in mid-January each year. Celebrating South Beach's architectural heritage for twenty years, participants have enjoyed a cornucopia of events: vintage film festivals, classic automobile rallies, big band concerts, the Moon Over Miami Ball and gala Ocean Drive street festivals.

## PAGE 153
### PARK CENTRAL HOTEL
640 Ocean Drive
The seven-story Park Central Hotel towers as a tribute to Henry Hohauser, one of Miami Beach's most prolific architects in the 1930's. An Art Deco gem erected in 1937, the Park Central displays stark geometric window patterns trimmed by stucco "eyebrows". The symmetrical facade is austere, highlighted by strong vertical bands and offset by streamlined curvature at the corners. New York restauranteur Tony Goldman handsomely renovated this Depression Moderne edifice during South Beach's recent, and glorious, rebirth.

## PAGE 159
### DECO LIFEGUARD STANDS
Uniquely simple, yet retro in design, Miami Beach's Deco lifeguard stands, built from designs submitted by local architects and artists, were installed from 1993 to 1995 as part of the beach restoration project. Inspired by a variety of themes, some quite nautical, the stands function perfectly.

## PAGE 160
### MIAMI BEACH PATROL BUILDING
Ocean Drive at 10th Street
Deco flourishes like porthole windows, a rounded semicircular facade and a roof balcony with a ship's railing distinguish the Miami Beach Patrol Building's classic Nautical Moderne construction. Created in 1939 by architect August Geiger, an associate of L. Murray Dixon, the utilitarian Patrol Building appears like a grand luxury liner set on land.

## PAGE 161A
### BEACON HOTEL
720 Ocean Drive
A premier hotel since the tourist heyday of the Thirties, the Beacon was designed by H. O. Nelson in 1936. The square facade is distinguished by a stepped parapet with vertical fluting. Bas relief Deco designs are etched, abstractly, into the exterior stucco. Originally a 66-room hotel, The Beacon offered the "American Plan"— breakfast, dinner and a room for $15 a day. During World War II, it, along with other Deco beauties, housed the U. S. Army's Air Force Technical Training Command.

## PAGE 161B
### HOTEL WEBSTER
1220 Collins Avenue
Stylized in 1936 by Henry Hohauser (1895-1963), one of Miami Beach's chief architects, the Webster buildings display an organic quality with deck-like balconies that sweep across the horizontal facades. Classically Moderne, the Art Deco details and tropical flourishes evoke an inestimable appeal and glamorous aura.

## PAGE 161C
### BREAKWATER
940 Ocean Drive
Architect Anton Skislewicz and builder Morris Alpert devised the U-shaped, 3-story Breakwater extravaganza in 1939. The quintessential Streamline edifice, constructed for $110,000, retains a grand Ocean Drive porch and original vertical neon sign. Scored stucco bands, like racing stripes, decorate the projecting facade giving an impression of speed and motion— themes from the Thirties. Cantilevered overhangs frame etched glass windows. The Breakwater was restored in the mid 1980's, and sits on the original site of Miami Beach's Strand Theater.

## PAGE 164, 166, 167
### GALLERY HOTEL
436 Ocean Drive
Designed by architect Albert Anis, a Chicagoan, (1889-1964), the 2-story, 5-bay building at 436 Ocean Drive originally opened as the Golden Hotel in 1936. Ben Golden built it for $35,000. Wall extensions with a faceted arch flank the entry, and abstract thunderbird design motifs, a derivative of the North American Indian culture, appear on the facade and parapet. Next door, at 444 Ocean Drive, an ornamental wrought iron balustrade and an open, tiled terrace run the length of the facade of Henry Hohauser's original 1936 Surf Hotel.

## PAGE 165
### FLAMINGO PLAZA
Meridian Avenue
Flamingo flourishes, etched onto glass and mortar, jazz up the entryways to Deco dreamlands—lending a spirit of the tropics, color, artistry and detailing to these remarkable, and historic, hotels and apartment dwellings.

## PAGE 168
### DELANO
1685 Collins Avenue
Like a twenty-first century space shuttle, the Delano, circa 1947, soars twelve flights, extending its fin-like towers skyward. Columbia-trained architect Robert Swartburg, a native of Romania, is credited with designing this stunning pastiche of octagonal motifs, an articulated central mass and multi-paned windows, corner set to capture the breezes sweeping off Miami Beach.

## PAGE 168
### NATIONAL
1677 Collins Avenue
Next to the Delano stands the National, a hotel that dates back to 1940. Its design, by architect Roy F. France, also the auteur of the St. Moritz, is influenced by the International Style, Cubism and the Bauhaus school. Exhibiting scored square patterns and a central vertical facade element, the Deco edifice is topped by a spherical cupola.

## PAGE 169
### RITZ PLAZA
1701 Collins Avenue
The 11-story, 132-room Ritz Plaza, one of the tallest Deco hotels, was erected in 1940, just prior to the onset of World War II. L. Murray Dixon, from Live Oak, Florida, became one of the most noted architects creating the fanciful, Busby Berkeley-inspired style on Miami Beach. The angular Ritz Plaza, newly restored and replete with wraparound windows, aerial spires, and a roof tower, symbolic of a periscope, is one of Dixon's signature buildings.

## PAGE 170
### STAR ISLAND
Star Island, situated off Miami Beach and east of Watson Island, is a man-made oasis, a result of the harbor dredging after the 1926 hurricane. Between MacArthur and Venetian Causeways three such spoil islands exist, providing sites for oceanfront villas for celebrities like Gloria Estefan and Don Johnson.

## PAGE 177
### NATION'S BANK TOWER
100 SE 2nd Street
I. M. Pei, a pre-eminent contemporary architect, designed this 47-story contemporary skyscraper, first known as the Centrust Building, in 1987. Brilliantly lit by hundreds of 1000-watt lamps, the multi-colored, off-changing illuminations soar into Miami's skyline. The commercial building contains 600,000 square feet of office space. The celebrated landscaped roof garden features a circular pool surrounded by pergolas.

## PAGE 185
### ORCHID
This spectacular bloom is a moth orchid, a type of phalaenopsis. Deriving its name from the Greek term "phaluna," or moth, the phalaenopsis is one of 18 genera of the Aerides tribe. The delicate flowers are shade loving, long bloomers particularly fond of Miami's tropical milieu.

## PAGE 185, 186, 187
### FAIRCHILD TROPICAL GARDEN
10901 Old Cutler Road
Fairchild Tropical Garden, a treasure of sub-tropical flora, encompasses 83 acres that integrate diverse botanical collections with topographical features. Based on a classic design created by landscape architect William Lyman Phillips in the 1930's, the Garden includes the Montgomery Palmetum, a signature exhibit of 800 species of palms, including more endangered palm species than all other botanical gardens in the world. Dedicated in 1938 by Colonel Robert M. Montgomery and named for horticulturist David Fairchild, a Department of Agriculture plant explorer, Fairchild Garden's endangered species collection includes 4,000 plantings of 100 endangered, threatened or rare species from South Florida's archipelago. The cycad collection, one of the world's rarest collections, holds more than 90 per cent of published species. Seedlings are propagated, and endangered plants are conserved in place. As a public botanical site, Fairchild Garden is unparalleled.

## PAGE 191
### CAMILLUS HOUSE
726 N. E. First Avenue
Since 1960 Camillus House, a privately funded organization, has provided meals, shelter and medical assistance for the homeless in Miami. The center's staff of eighty, helped by constant private donations, supplies needed services for drug rehabilitation, physical therapy, employment training, transportation needs and other emergency requirements.

## PAGE 193
### BANYAN TREE
The lofty banyan, a type of ficus or fig tree with multiple trunks, is native to Madagascar. Pillar roots descend into the earth from the main trunk, creating a spectacular system of aerial roots. Superb examples of the banyan, India's sacred tree, frequent Miami's sub-tropical landscape.

## PAGE 196, 197
### MACARTHUR CAUSEWAY
Named for General Douglas MacArthur, the MacArthur Causeway connects Greater Miami to Miami Beach, spanning Biscayne Bay.

## REFERENCES TO SPECIFIC LOCATIONS

### BAL HARBOUR
The open-air shops at Bal Harbour, too marvelous to be called a "mall," may well be the most elegant collection of both fashion and flesh in the country. Bal Harbour Shops has gained the enviable distinction as one of the most prestigious fashion meccas in the world. The village itself is perfectly manicured, boasting ocean-front condominiums, and precious enough to have its own police force.

### BRICKELL AVENUE
William B. Brickell, for whom Brickell Avenue is named, opened Brickell's Trading Post, a supply center for early pioneer residents and Indians at the south bank of the Miami River, in 1871. Along modern-day Brickell Avenue, perhaps Miami's most impressive boulevard, clusters of international financial institutions, high-rises and condominiums parade. Acclaimed local architectural firms such as Arquitectonica have punctuated the Miami Skyline with colorful, strikingly inventive and thoroughly contemporary structures.

### CALLE OCHO
Calle Ocho, the Spanish name for S. W. Eighth Street, runs like an artery through the heart of Little Havana. A trip along Calle Ocho, stretching from Brickell Avenue through downtown, encounters head-on aspects of Cuba's traditional culture: Cuban coffee stands, shops and eateries dishing up moros y cristianos or arroz con pollo; Spanish-speaking neighborhoods; patriotic memorials; the Cuban Museum of Arts and Culture. Little Havana is home to a quarter million exiled Cubans.

### CARD SOUND ROAD
Scenic vistas en route to the Florida Keys from Miami are best captured along the less traveled Card Sound Road. The two-lane road takes a little longer, but nature's grandeur—watery mangroves and native hardwood hammocks—are close by. Cross the Card Sound Bridge and the roadway merges with Route 1 at Mile Marker #109. Key West lies at the end of the Florida keys' archipelago.

### COCONUT GROVE
The area's original pioneer settlement on Biscayne Bay, Coconut Grove began as a winter retreat for wealthy northern tourists. For $100 Charles and Jack Peacock purchased Anna Beaseley's 31-acre homestead and erected the Bay View House for lodgers. Ralph Munroe, an architect and photographer, was a catalyst for the community's founding. Interestingly, by several accounts, only two coconut trees flourished at what came to be called "Coconut Grove." A century later "The Grove," as it is affectionately known, has preserved its singular allure, enhanced recently by upscale galleries, smart cafes, colorful festivals and always, fascinating characters.

### COLLINS AVENUE
Traveling the main artery along Miami Beach, images from the Fifties, the era when Miami became Vacationland, U.S.A., may surface. Nearly a half century later, however, vintage resorts like the Fontainebleau, Eden Roc and Sans Souci have undergone multi-million dollar facelifts; and thousands of condominiums front the wide, sandy beaches.

### CORAL GABLES
"A City Beautiful" was the apt motto ascribed to Coral Gables by George Merrick, its founder and designer. Merrick, an idealist and a visionary with a calling as a town planner, incorporated his model city in 1925, spending nearly $100 million during the Florida boom era. He cast its architecture with a European theme. Coral Gables endures today as one man's tribute to Mediterranean Revivalism, a romantic building style laced with Spanish and Italian overtones. A model of American urban planning, Coral Gables is distinguished by its town plazas and fountains, wide boulevards, intricate waterways, ornate civic statuary, and elegant residential and commercial edifices.

### DOWNTOWN
Miami's meteoric passage from swamplands and palmetto scrub to its place as a New World Center occurred in less than a century. The rise of its skyline, fast-paced traffic corridors, high-rise contemporary buildings, array of cultural amenities and facilities and international cruise port followed the recession of the 1970's. Stops along downtown Miami's palm-laden trail to urban cosmopolitanism include: Metro-Dade Cultural Center, the Historical Museum of Southern Florida, the Center for Fine Arts, Gusman Theater for the Performing Arts, Miami Arena and Bayfront Park.

### FLORIDA CITY
Known as the "winter vegetable capital," Florida City, just off U.S. Route 1, is home to spacious farmlands where avocados, tomatoes, limes, cucumbers, strawberries and more are picked and trucked nationwide. A century ago, Flagler's train tracks reached Homestead in 1903, en route to the Florida East Coast Railroad's Key West terminus in January, 1912.

### HOMESTEAD
Homestead traces its beginnings to Henry Flagler's decision to extend the Florida East Coast Railway south to Miami and ultimately to Key West. The pioneer railroad town, incorporated in 1913, has triumphed over major hurricanes in 1926, 1935 and 1945, and has survived, and been redefined, following the severe impact of Hurricane Andrew. The historic business district is currently witnessing a revitalization.

### KEY BISCAYNE
Key Biscayne, a fragile microcosm of coastal Florida itself, is America's southernmost barrier island. A long litany of people have called it home. For the Tequesta Indians the clear waters around Key Biscayne proved to be a magnet for fishing; to exlporer Ponce de Leon, the sandy isle became yet another discovery in 1513, and he named it Santa Maria; for William S. Harney, it served as a military base during the Seminole Wars; to William J. Matheson, 1,700 acres of Key Biscayne became known as "Matheson's Island," which became a center for experimental cultivation of tropical plants. In 1940 prime lands from the Matheson estate, encompassing two miles of Atlantic beach, were donated as a public park.

### LIBERTY CITY
Like many urban centers, Miami's northwest inner city has witnessed a dire transformation. In 1937 the federal Public Works Administration, with the support of Miami's Negro Civic League, built Liberty Square, Florida's first housing project, near Liberty City. Over the span of fifty years, however, Liberty City evolved to a poverty-stricken ghetto, and violent race riots erupted in 1968 and 1980. Recently local leaders and private capital have paved the way to rebuild the community's housing, shopping and educational centers.

### LITTLE HAVANA
Little Havana, Miami's Cuban quarter, has seen an explosion of culture as the waves of refugees, stowaways and new arrivals have planted their traditions, language, art and ethos in their new homeland. From the 3,000 "flights to freedom" from 1965 to 1973, to the freedom flotilla of homemade rafts in 1980, bringing 125,000 Marielitos, the Hispanic population of Miami has mushroomed to a quarter million.

### MIAMI BEACH
A barrier island stretching seven miles along the Atlantic, Miami Beach embraces seven square miles of land, bordered by a magnificent 300-foot wide white sand beach. Spawned by John S. Collins' 1896 avocado plantation and his discovery of a fresh water aquifer, Miami Beach development commenced—a subdivision was platted on July 9, 1912 by J. N. Lummus. The city, with 33 voters, was incorporated in 1915. A bridge connected the island to the mainland, and one of the country's most popular recreational spots, no longer "Collins' Folly," was born.

### OCEAN DRIVE
South Beach's main drag, Ocean Drive, is an everchanging pageant—pink Thunderbirds from the Fifties, preserved Deco hotels like pastel confections, swarms of on-lookers, swank clubs and stylish cafes—all parade non-stop along the beachfront drive. Transformed from a seedy, forgotten route, highlighted by an ageing population and decaying hotels, Ocean Drive has witnessed a resplendent rebirth—as a glamour destination for fashion photographers, international jet-setters, trend-setting film stars, and having as its centerpiece the twentieth century's finest collection of Art Deco and Streamline architecture.

### REDLANDS
Redlands, a community originated at the turn of the century by hardy pioneers willing to farm the red soil, stands as a lasting tribute to an almost forgotten way of life. Theirs was a simple, hardy existence; raising avocados, pineapples and limes, and building unpretentious, wooden porch-lined cottages, a small town inn at Anderson's Corner, and the turn-of-the-century Richmond Inn. The tiny municipality, recovering from the devastation visited by Hurricane Andrew in 1992, survives.

### SOUTH BEACH
The epicenter of Miami Beach, newly restored and revitalized with a pastiche all its own, SoBe, as South Beach is familiarly termed, has evolved as a tropical version of SoHo. Exteriors of pink, aqua and green set against the brilliant azure sky create a stageset for this international destination—America's new Riviera.

## CREDITS

Photography, page layout and captions . . . . . . . . . . . . Alan S. Maltz

Text  . . . . . . . . . . . . . . . . . . . . . . . . . . . . . . . . . . . . Les Standiford

Graphic Design  . . . . . . . . . . . . . . . . . . . . . . . . . . . . Robert Bender

Commentary  . . . . . . . . . . . . . . . . . . . . . . . . . . . . . Sharon L. Wells

Creative Consultant  . . . . . . . . . . . . . . . . . . . . . . . . Leslie C. Artigue

## ACKNOWLEDGEMENTS

My heartfelt gratitude and appreciation go out to the following talented and dedicated individuals:

My wife Leslie — for whose love, devotion, inspiration and creative input I am always grateful.

Aunt May — for her unconditional love, her inspiration, her heart and her soul.

Robert Bender of Creative Services— for his friendship, his relentless pursuit of perfection and for sincerely caring.

Edward Sharp — whose long-term friendship, inspiration, generosity and hospitality will not go without mention.

Ursula Boll — for her friendship, her encouragement, her inspiration and her help with pre-publication sales.

Steve Hooper of TIEN WAH Press — for his guidance and assistance through the pre-press process.

John Ribbler of John Ribbler Associates — for his input and assistance throughout this project.

Daniel Balbi of Creative Services — for his incomparable digital color work.

I would like to offer my sincere thanks to Merrett Stierheim and everyone at the Greater Miami Convention and Visitors Bureau for their support and enthusiasm throughout the creation of *Miami City of Dreams.*

Lastly, I would like to acknowledge those who made special efforts in arranging photo shoots, so vital to the content of the finished work.  They are:

Holly Blount  *Vizcaya*
Nancy Brown  *Friends of the Everglades*
Lou Anne Colodny  *Museum of Contemporary Art*
Stephanie Kirby  *Biltmore Hotel*
Enid Rosenthal  *Bal Harbour Shops*
Laurette Sapah-Gulian  *Dade County Youth Fair*
Rebecca Vazquez  *Winthrop Management*
Vicki Vigorito  *Miami City Ballet*

## TECHNICAL NOTES

Most of the images included in *Miami City of Dreams* were captured as I drove randomly through different areas of the city between the hours of sunrise to 10am and 4pm to sunset.
The 35mm format best suits the spontaneous nature of my style.  I choose Nikon equipment.
My lighting is simple: either natural or natural with strobe.  My film of choice is Fujichrome Velvia.

*Any further questions on technique may be directed to the publisher.*